Yuck, That's Gross!

WORLD BOOK

Introduction

Nature is filled with some amazing creatures. From ocean bottoms to mountain tops, from hot deserts to freezing tundra, the *Ugh! Yuck! and Whoa!* books highlight the most extreme animals: the rudest, the deadliest, the strangest, and the ugliest! This book is all about animals that behave badly. You'll learn about animals that eat the freakiest foods, animals that play with poo, and animals with other yucky habits! These habits are often **adaptations.** An **adaptation** is something an animal or other living thing has or does that helps it survive and **reproduce** (make more living things like itself) in its environment. Read on to see some of the grossest and strangest animal behaviors. This Yuck Factor meter will show how gross each animal is!

RABBIT

Rabbits eat plants, and plants are
hard to **digest** (get energy from).
So rabbits eat their food twice!
Rabbits make two kinds of poo:
soft pellets, or small lumps, which
they eat again, and solid pellets, which they
don't. Rabbits eat their own poo to **digest** it
again to get all the energy
out of it they can!

WOOD LOUSE

These little bugs, sometimes called "pill bugs" or "roly-polies," live in gross places. They like their homes to be dark, damp, and warm. Yuck! You can find wood lice under stones and in the bark of trees.

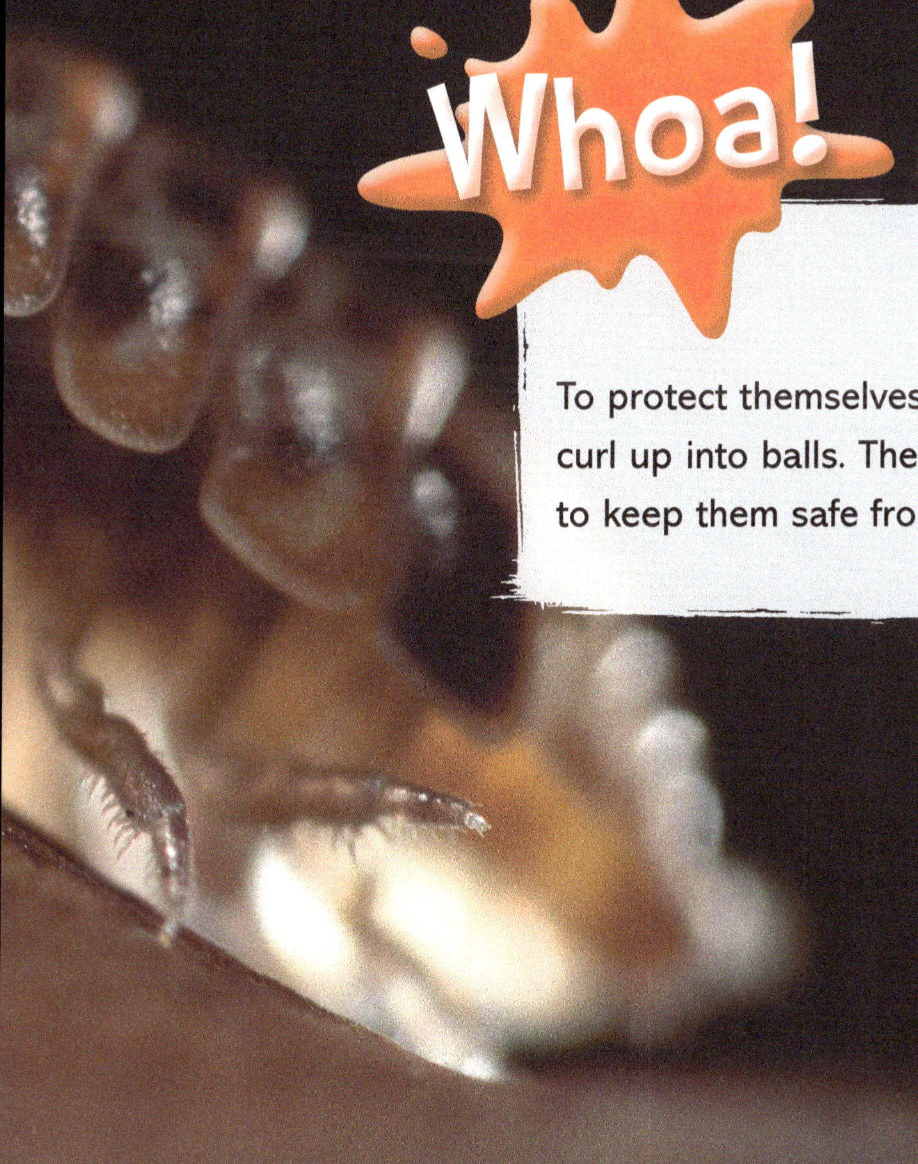

To protect themselves, some wood lice curl up into balls. Their hard shells help to keep them safe from harm.

VULTURE

Vultures mainly eat **carrion** *(KAR ee uhn,* dead and decaying animal flesh). One type of vulture, called the bearded vulture, mostly eats animal bones! It can swallow bones whole. If a bone is too big to eat, the bearded vulture carries it high up in the air and drops it on rocks below to break it apart.

Yuckiest Foods

Jackal

Jackals are **scavengers**. They eat the bodies of dead animals that they find!

Herring gull

These birds will eat almost anything—even scraps of garbage!

Goliath birdeater

This huge spider gets its
name from being able to eat
small birds!

Goat

Some people say goats
eat tin cans! That's not
quite true. But goats are
very curious, and they are
often drawn to the smells
of tin cans and other food
containers. They might eat
cardboard, paper, or other
trash!

HAGFISH

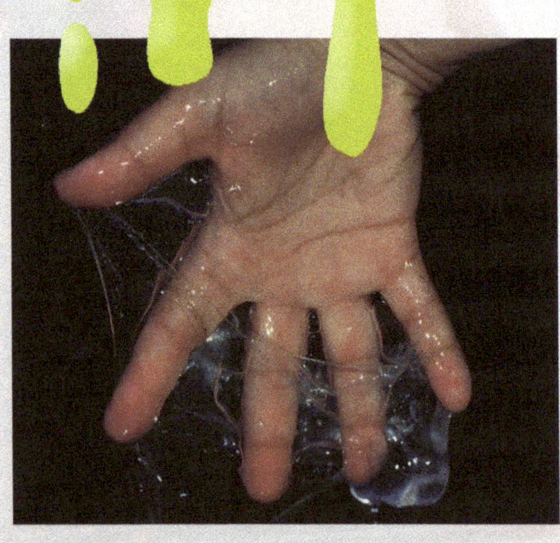

Hagfish can get really slimy really fast. In just one minute, they can make enough slime to fill up a bucket!

Hagfish are long, skinny fish that live deep in the sea. When it is threatened, a hagfish makes a lot of slime to keep its **predators** away!

HIPPOPOTAMUS

A male hippopotamus *(HIHP uh POT uh muhs)* uses his poo to get a date with a female hippo! He spins his tail around to throw his poo far and wide.

YUCK FACTOR
HIGH

GECKO

Most geckos don't have eyelids. Instead, a gecko's eye is protected by a clear membrane *(MEHM brayn*, a thin layer) that doesn't move. The gecko keeps these membranes clean by licking them!

BURYING
BEETLE

Burying beetles use the bodies of small, dead animals like mice and birds to **reproduce.** The beetles dig around and under the dead animal. Once the body is in the hole, a female burying beetle lays her eggs in it! The baby beetles will use the body as food.

MARABOU
STORK

This big bird is a **scavenger**. A **scavenger** eats animals that are dead. Marabou storks do not have feathers on their heads and necks so they can dig around in their food more easily. Marabou storks mainly eat the meat of dead animals…as well as their poo! Yuck!

GIRAFFE

Giraffes are known for their long necks. They also have huge, blue tongues! To get their food down, giraffes need a lot of saliva. (Saliva is the wet, sticky stuff in our mouths.) These messy eaters often drool all over!

YUCK FACTOR
LOW

DUNG BEETLE

This kind of beetle eats animal poo, called **dung**. Some **dung** beetles, called dwellers, live in and on **dung** piles. Others, called rollers, roll balls of **dung** to use for food or as a place to lay eggs. **Dung** beetles called tunnelers move **dung** into tunnels that they dig in the ground. They use the **dung** as a place to lay eggs.

PANDA

Male giant pandas do handstands when they pee! Like many animals, the male giant panda uses his pee to mark his territory. The higher up the pee, the farther its smell carries on the breeze. To spray his pee as high up possible, the male giant panda will stand on his hands and pee on a tree! This tells other male pandas to keep out.

SEA CUCUMBER

These sea animals have long, fleshy bodies that look a bit like cucumbers. To keep safe from attackers, sea cucumbers can throw their guts outside their bodies! **Predators** can get tangled in sea cucumbers' sticky organs, and the sea cucumber gets away. Then, sea cucumbers grow new guts.

YUCK FACTOR
HIGH

SURINAM TOAD

The Surinam toad has a yucky
appearance. It has small eyes,
no tongue, and no teeth. But it is
especially known for the unusual way
it raises its young. Most frogs lay
eggs in the water. These eggs hatch
into tadpoles that later become frogs.
A Surinam toad mother carries her
eggs in the spongy skin on her back.
The young do not leave her skin until
they have grown into tiny toads, more
than two months after they hatch.

YUCK FACTOR
MEDIUM

PEARLFISH

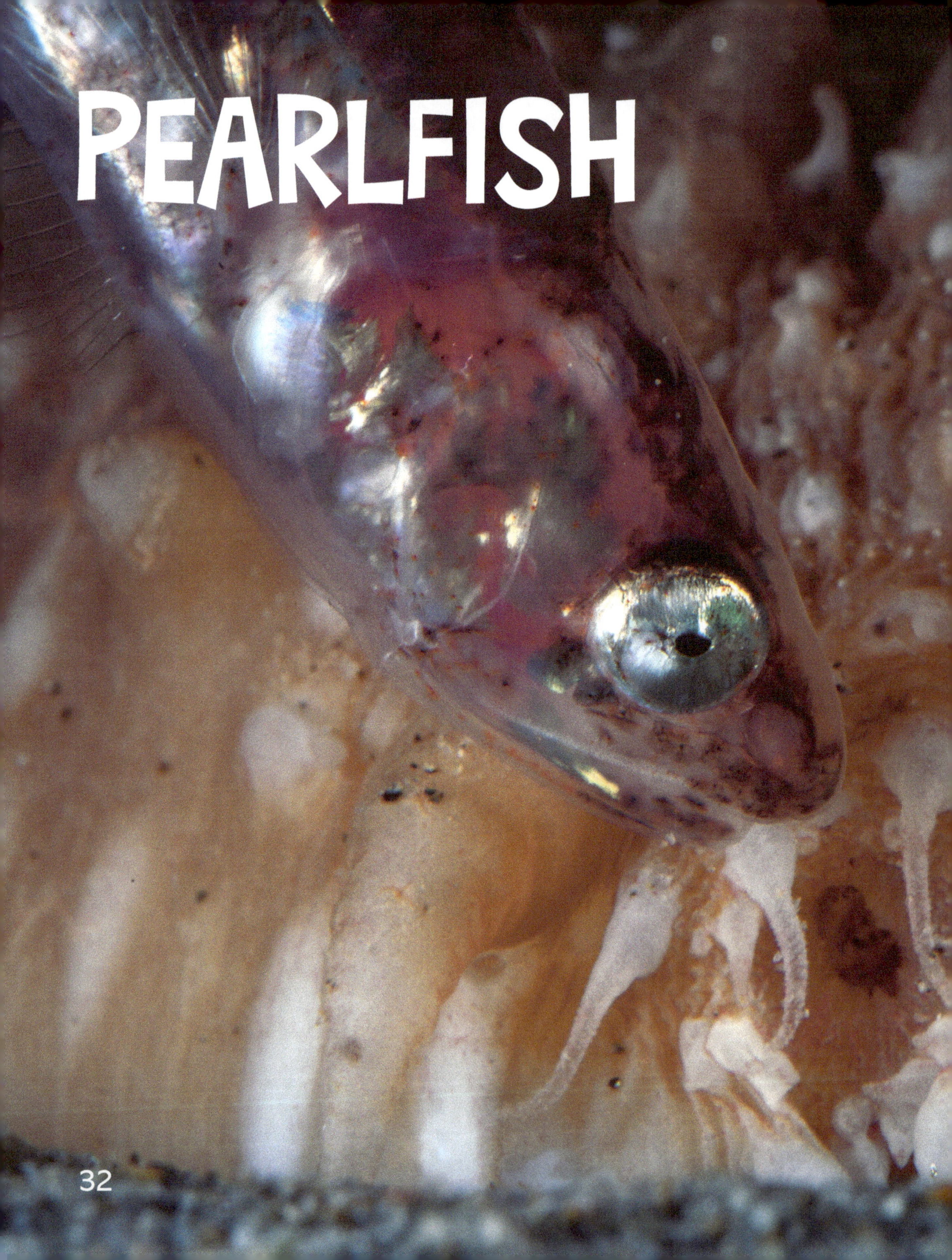

There is something else gross about sea cucumbers. Little fish called pearlfish sometimes lives inside sea cucumbers' guts to keep safe! Some pearlfish munch on the sea cucumber's internal organs—which, of course, grow back!

This pearlfish is peeking its head out of a sea cucumber's bottom.

CATTLE

Cattle are big animals. Bulls (male cattle) weigh more than 2,000 pounds! They eat a lot of food. **Digesting** a lot of food makes a lot of waste. It can also make a lot of gas—and not the kind we pump into cars! Cattle burp and "pass" so much gas (yes, what a rude person would call fart) that it affects our climate! The gas from cattle adds to the other gases in the air that cause global warming.

YUCK FACTOR
MEDIUM

FLY

Flies are insects with strong wings. They can be dangerous pests. They carry germs inside their bodies, on the tip of their mouthparts, and in the hair on their bodies. When a fly "bites," or when it touches any object, it leaves some of these germs behind. Flies carry germs that can cause serious diseases in people and other animals.

GIANT SALAMANDER

Salamanders are animals that look a bit like lizards. But they are actually more closely related to frogs. Giant salamanders spend their whole lives swimming through the water. Giant salamander dads are in charge of watching over the eggs that the mother salamander lays. The dads may eat some of the eggs! They seem to eat the ones that look unhealthy to be sure that their salamander babies that do hatch are strong.

YUCK FACTOR
MEDIUM

ZOMBIE WORM

Zombie people like to eat brains, and zombie worms have a strange appetite, too. Zombie worms stay in place—like plants—on the bones of dead ocean animals like whales. They use a chemical called an acid to break down the bones. Then, zombie worms feed the soft stuff inside the bones to tiny living things called bacteria that live inside the worms. Then, they eat these bacteria!

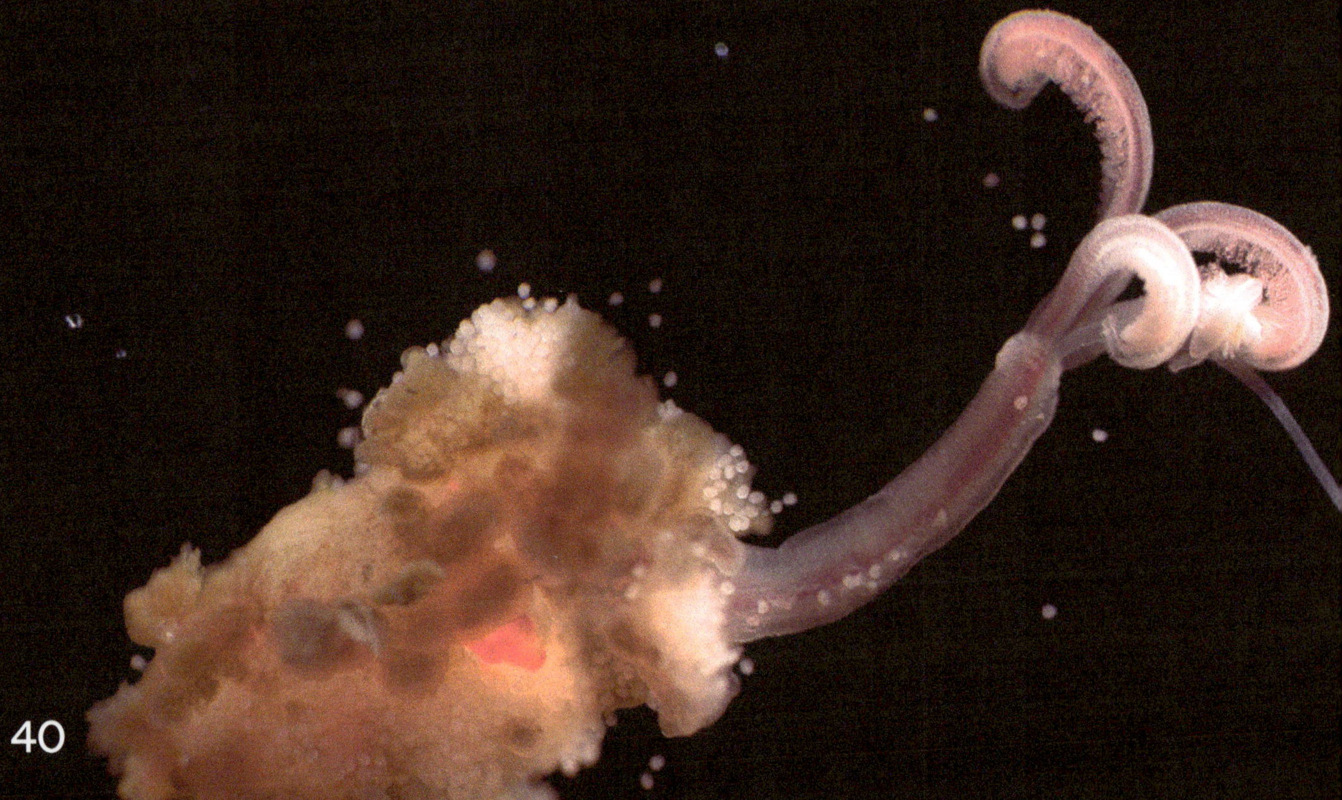

YUCK FACTOR
HIGH

Cannibal Animals

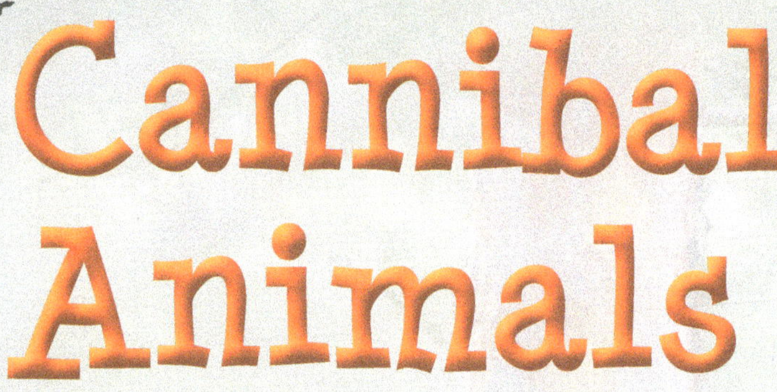

Cannibalism *(KAN uh buh LIHZ uhm)* is when an animal eats animals like itself. Yuck!

Praying mantis

Female praying mantises sometimes eat their mates. The male can continue to move for a short time even after his head has been eaten!

Black widow

Black widow spiders got their name because females often kill and eat their mates!

King cobra

The king cobra is called the king because it hunts and eats other types of snakes!

Humboldt squid

These squids can get angry when they are eating. If another squid gets close, they'll eat the other squid!

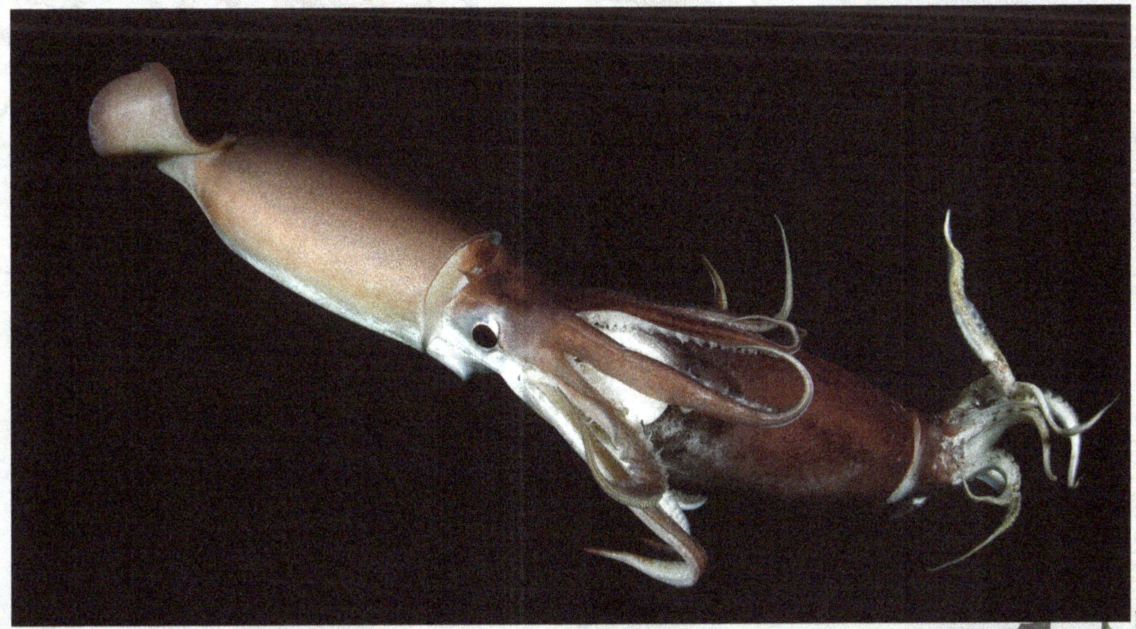

HYENA

This hyena cub is playing with a gross toy. That's a pile of dried-up elephant poo! Yuck!

Some monkeys play with poo, too! This monkey is digging around elephant poo to pick out seeds to eat.

Glossary

Adaptation

a change in structure, form, or habits to fit different conditions.

Cannibal

an animal that eats others of its own kind.

Carrion

the flesh of a dead animal.

Digest

to break down food in the mouth, stomach, and intestines so that it can be used by the body.

Dung

waste matter from the intestines of animals; droppings.

Predator

an animal that hunts, kills, and eats other animals.

Reproduce

to bear young; to create offspring.

Scavenger

an animal that feeds on the bodies of dead animals.

Index

Acknowledgments

Cover: © Andy Rouse, Nature Picture Library; © Neil Aldridge, Nature Picture Library

4-5 © Rolf Nussbaumer, Nature Picture Library; © Laurie Campbell, Nature Picture Library

6-7 © Solvin Zankl, Nature Picture Library; © Shutterstock

8-9 © David Tipling, Nature Picture Library

10-11 © Nick Upton, Nature Picture Library; © Anup Shah, Nature Picture Library; © Andrew Snyder, MYN/Nature Picture Library; © Clare Malley, iStockphoto

12-13 © Visuals Unlimited/Nature Picture Library; © Brandon Cole, Nature Picture Library

14-15 © Denis-Huot/Nature Picture Library

16-17 © Michael D. Kern, Nature Picture Library

18-19 © ARCO/Nature Picture Library; © Andy Sands, Nature Picture Library

20-21 © Anup Shah, Nature Picture Library

22-23 © Andy Rouse, Nature Picture Library

24-25 © Neil Aldridge, Nature Picture Library

26-27 © Will Burrard-Lucas, Nature Picture Library

28-29 © David Fleetham, Nature Picture Library

30-31 © Tom McHugh, Science Source

32-33 © Jordi Chias, Nature Picture Library

34-35 © Gozzoli/Shutterstock

36-37 © Andy Sands, Nature Picture Library

38-39 © Yukihiro Fukuda, Nature Picture Library

40-41 © Natural History Museum London; Norio Miyamoto, Naturwissenschaften

42-43 © Mark Hamblin, 2020VISION/Nature Picture Library; © Visuals Unlimited/Nature Picture Library; © Jose B. Ruiz, Nature Picture Library; © Sandesh Kadur, Nature Picture Library; © Franco Banfi, Nature Picture Library

44-45 © Tina Malfilatre, Biosphoto/Alamy Images; © Steve Brigman, Shutterstock